ROMAN MYTHS

Kathy Elgin

W

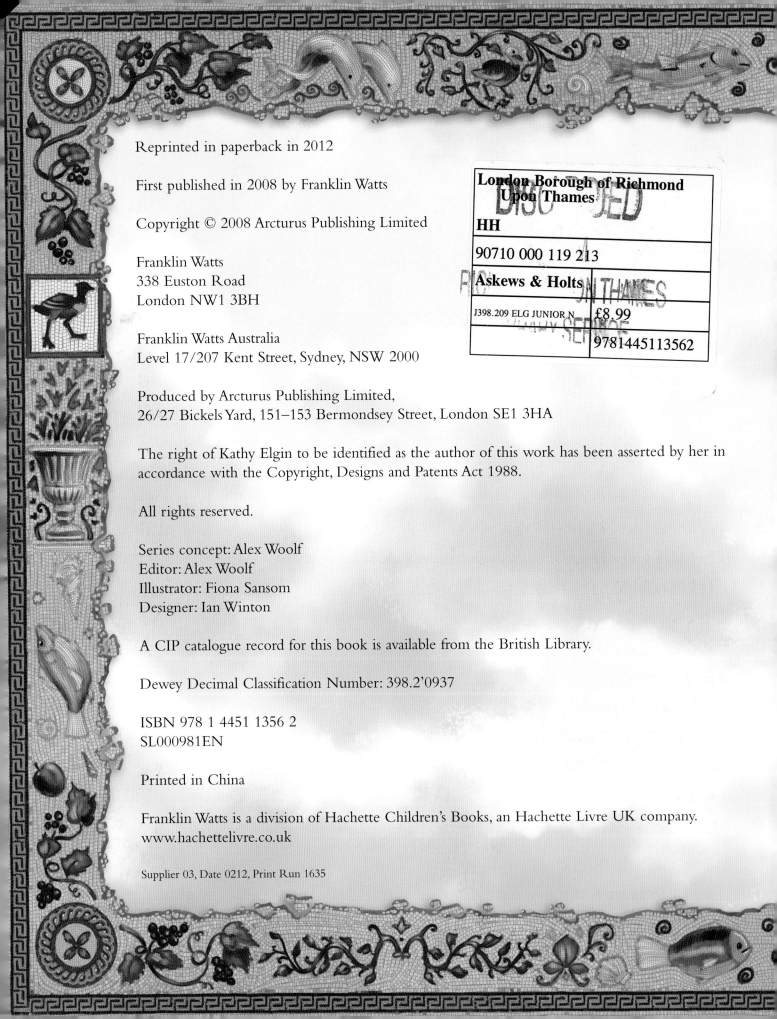

Reprinted in paperback in 2012

First published in 2008 by Franklin Watts

Copyright © 2008 Arcturus Publishing Limited

Franklin Watts
338 Euston Road
London NW1 3BH

Franklin Watts Australia
Level 17/207 Kent Street, Sydney, NSW 2000

Produced by Arcturus Publishing Limited,
26/27 Bickels Yard, 151–153 Bermondsey Street, London SE1 3HA

Series concept: Alex Woolf
Editor: Alex Woolf
Illustrator: Fiona Sansom
Designer: Ian Winton

A CIP catalogue record for this book is available from the British Library.

Dewey Decimal Classification Number: 398.2'0937

ISBN 978 1 4451 1356 2
SL000981EN

Printed in China

Franklin Watts is a division of Hachette Children's Books, an Hachette Livre UK company.
www.hachettelivre.co.uk

Supplier 03, Date 0212, Print Run 1635

CONTENTS

INTRODUCTION

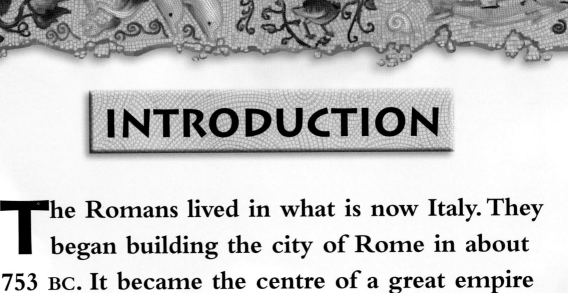

The Romans lived in what is now Italy. They began building the city of Rome in about 753 BC. It became the centre of a great empire (see right) that lasted until the fifth century AD.

SPIRITS AND SACRIFICES

The Romans worshipped many gods. The earliest ones were nature spirits who lived in springs, rivers and forests. These places were sacred and people were rather afraid of them. The Romans offered sacrifices of people to keep the gods happy.

MYTHS AND STORIES

Later, the Romans invented stories to explain things about the world around them. They made the gods responsible for the weather, the changing seasons and how well the crops grew. Other stories tried to explain how the world was created.

LONDON

NIMES

ROME
POMPEII

BYZANTIUM

CARTHAGE

MEDITERRANEAN SEA

ALEXANDRIA

The Romans inherited some of their gods from the Etruscans, a people who had lived in Italy some time earlier. The Romans also adopted gods from the countries they conquered, especially Greece. They gave the Greek gods new names and changed the stories slightly to make them more relevant to their own traditions.

FOUNDING MYTHS

The Romans also invented myths to explain how their own civilization had begun. In these stories, the gods are responsible for the founding of Rome. This made it appear that Rome was the greatest city on earth, and the Romans were the most powerful people. These tales were written down by a poet called Virgil (70-19 BC).

JUST LIKE PEOPLE

The Romans thought of their gods as living beings. They were related to each other just like human families. They *behaved* like humans, too. They fell in love, argued and became jealous or angry. They played tricks on each other and took revenge. They also appeared among mortals and interfered with their lives. When this happened, there was usually trouble.

The adventures of the gods and heroes were recorded in statues, wall paintings, and mosaics. You can still see many of these in Italy today. You can also see the Pantheon, the great temple in Rome, sacred to all the gods.

SATURN THE ANCIENT GOD

Saturn was the son of the chief of the Titans. They were a race of godlike giants. Saturn overthrew his father and became king. During Saturn's reign, the earth was peaceful and fertile. People called this 'the golden age'.

Saturn was afraid that one of his own sons would overthrow him. As each one was born, Saturn killed and ate it. But when the sixth son, Jupiter, was born, Saturn's wife hid him away. She gave Saturn a stone wrapped in a shawl instead. Jupiter grew up in secret on the island of Crete.

Eventually, Jupiter did overthrow his father. Saturn fled to Italy to escape his son's anger.

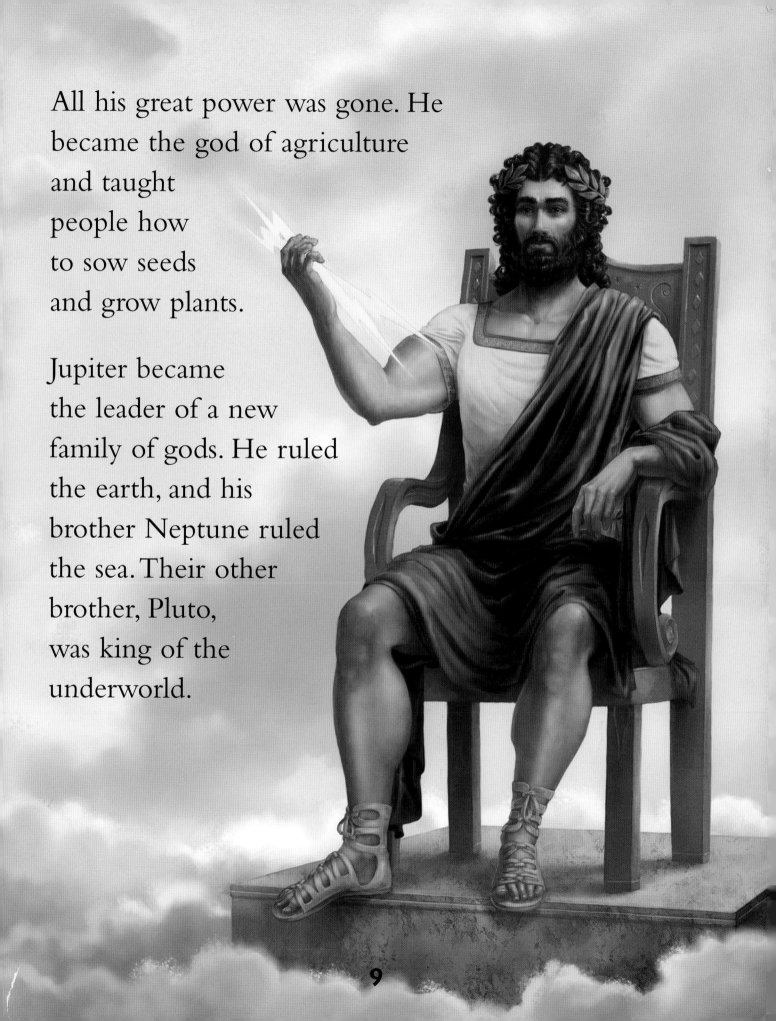

All his great power was gone. He
became the god of agriculture
and taught
people how
to sow seeds
and grow plants.

Jupiter became
the leader of a new
family of gods. He ruled
the earth, and his
brother Neptune ruled
the sea. Their other
brother, Pluto,
was king of the
underworld.

VENUS, VULCAN AND A MORTAL

The most beautiful of the goddesses was Venus, the goddess of love. She was married to the god Vulcan, who was a blacksmith and very ugly. Although he loved her, she did not like him at all. She was in love with Mars, the god of war. When Vulcan found out about this, he made a net of steel in his blacksmith's forge. Next time Mars and Venus met, he caught them in his net and chased Mars away.

Then Venus fell in love with the mortal Anchises, who lived in the city of Troy.

They had a son, Aeneas. Being the goddess of love, Venus did not want people to know that she loved an ordinary human. She made Anchises promise that he would never tell the boy who his mother was.

When the Greeks declared war on Troy, Venus was afraid for her mortal family. She visited Aeneas in a dream and warned him to leave the city. Aeneas escaped with his father, wife and son.

THE VOYAGES OF AENEAS

Aeneas left Troy with his father, Anchises, his wife, and their little son. As they crept away from the city, his wife Creusa was lost. That night, her ghost visited Aeneas. She told him that the gods meant him to found a great empire in a foreign country.

They found a ship and set sail. Because Aeneas was half-god, half-mortal, the gods looked after him. But some, like Juno, were envious and tried to harm him. Juno raised a storm to wreck their ship, but Neptune rescued them. They were cast ashore near Carthage in North Africa.

Here Aeneas fell in love with Dido, the queen of that country. They were very happy. Life was so pleasant that Aeneas forgot all about his mission. Jupiter sent Mercury, the messenger god, to remind him.

Aeneas set sail again and left Dido behind. Full of sorrow, she killed herself. She made a great funeral fire and threw herself onto it. After many other adventures, Aeneas landed in Italy.

AENEAS IN THE UNDERWORLD

Old Anchises had died during the long voyage. When Aeneas landed in Italy, he decided to visit the underworld. This was where people went when they died. He wanted to see his father one last time. It was a dangerous journey. He made an offering to the gods. Then his mother Venus turned herself into a dove and led him on his way.

First he came to the cave of sleep and death. It was guarded by two giants, but Aeneas passed safely through. Next, he reached the River Lethe. The souls of the dead had to cross this river in a ferryboat.

Charon the ferryman rowed Aeneas to the other side. There stood the giant three-headed dog, Cerberus. He was the guardian of the underworld. Cerberus growled but let Aeneas pass. Because he was half-god, the monsters could not harm him.

At last Aeneas found his father. He did not look old and ill any more. He smiled to see his son. The souls of other dead friends were also there. Aeneas saw his wife, and Dido, and many famous people.

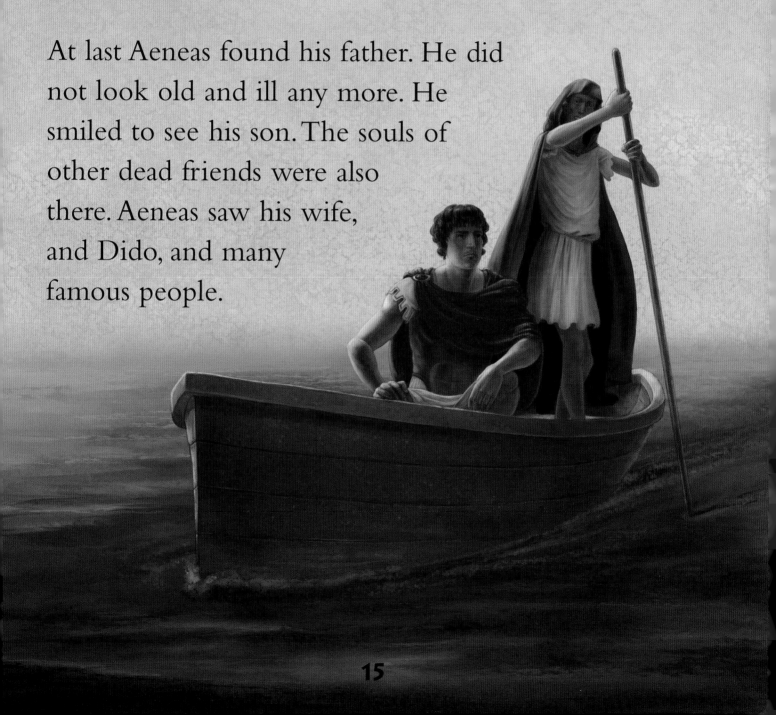

Finally Aeneas said goodbye and travelled on. He soon found himself in the open air near the River Tiber. By the river was a beautiful girl. She was Lavinia, the king's daughter.

Legend said that Lavinia would marry a stranger and make her country great. Aeneas married Lavinia and they built a town called Lavinium. In time, Rome was built in the same place.

GANYMEDE

Ganymede was the son of the King of Troy. He was a beautiful boy with golden hair.

One day, Jupiter saw him walking in the mountains. He changed himself into an eagle, swooped down and carried the boy off. In exchange, he left two magic horses for the boy's father.

Ganymede became Jupiter's servant. His job was to pour wine for the gods. Jupiter also made a picture of the boy in shining stars. This can still be seen in the sky today.

ROMULUS AND REMUS

Amulius, a descendant of Aeneas, overthrew his brother Numitor and became king in his place. But Numitor had a daughter, Rea Silva. If she had a son, he would certainly grow up to avenge his grandfather. Amulius forced Rea to become a vestal virgin in the temple, so she could never marry and have children.

One night the god Mars visited Rea and she gave birth to twin sons. When Amulius discovered this he snatched them away. He ordered his soldiers to throw them into the River Tiber. But a big wave washed the babies out of the water.

A she-wolf discovered them lying on the river bank. She took them home to her den and

suckled them along with her own cubs. The
boys grew strong and healthy.

One day a shepherd called Faustulus found the
twins and took them home. His wife Larentia
knew they had been sent by the gods. She
brought them up as their own children and
named them Romulus and Remus.

HOW ROME WAS BUILT

The two boys grew into fine young men. Remus was stronger than anybody else, and Romulus could run very fast.

One day Remus was captured by strangers. They took him to the local landowner. Remus did not know that this was Numitor, his grandfather. But Numitor saw that the boy looked like his daughter Rea. He welcomed the two boys as his grandsons. Together, they raised an army against Amulius. They defeated him and won back their kingdom.

Romulus and Remus began to build the new city of Rome. But they could not agree about where to put it. There were seven hills in the area. Romulus wanted to build on the Palatine Hill. Remus preferred the Aventine.

Romulus started building walls. Remus made fun of his brother because the walls were so low. He jumped over them, laughing. Angrily, Romulus turned on his brother and hit him. Remus fell dead. As soon as he had done this, Romulus was sorry. But it was too late.

THE SABINE WOMEN

Romulus finished building the new city. He named it Rome, after himself. He brought all his soldiers and friends to live in it. But he had forgotten something. All the men wanted to get married, but there were hardly any women.

Romulus had to find wives from somewhere. He ordered a great feast and invited the men of a neighbouring tribe, the Sabines. While the men were away, Roman soldiers invaded the Sabine city. They captured all the women and took them back to Rome.

The Sabine men were furious. They declared war on Rome. But many of the Sabine women had grown to love their new husbands. In the middle of the battle, they ran between the two armies and begged them to stop fighting. So Romulus and Titus, king of the Sabines, made peace and ruled together for many years.

When Titus died, Romulus ruled alone. One day he disappeared in a thunderstorm. The gods had taken him up to heaven to live with them.

NUMA POMPILIUS, THE RELUCTANT KING

After Romulus died, the Romans chose Numa Pompilius for their second king. He was a quiet man who lived in the country. He loved reading and studying. He did not want to give up his happy life to rule the warlike Romans.

He agreed to be king only if the gods wanted it. The priests dressed him in special robes and said a prayer. They waited for a sign from the gods.

Suddenly there was thunder and lightning. A splendid shield fell from the sky. On it, Jupiter had written a prophecy about the future of Rome. Numa knew that he must now be king. To thank Jupiter, he had eleven other shields made. Every year the priests carried the twelve sacred shields through the city in a procession.

Numa became a great king, famous for his wisdom. He improved the calendar, dividing the year into twelve months. He gave people holidays and made their lives better. After a long reign, he died peacefully of old age.

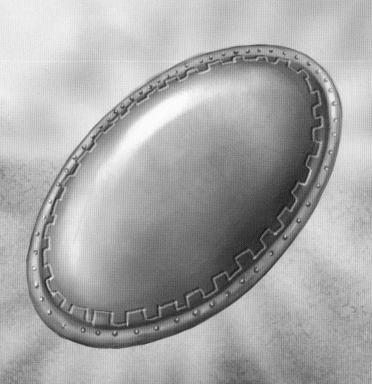

JANUS AND CARNA

The god Janus had two faces, which looked in opposite directions. One had a beard while the other was clean-shaven. January is named after Janus because this month looks back at the old year and forward to the new one. Janus watched over Rome. During peacetime, the doors to his temple were kept shut. When the city was at war, however, the doors were opened so that he could protect the city.

Janus loved a nymph called Carna. He made her the goddess of doorways. Her special plant was whitethorn, which kept evil spirits away. It was especially powerful against witches who came in the night to suck the blood of babies.

There was a woman whose baby daughter had been attacked by witches. Everyone could see the scratches on the child's cheeks. Carna went to her house. She touched the doorposts with whitethorn and put a sprig of it in the window. The witches were unable to pass the magic plant, and the child was saved.

TARQUIN THE PROUD AND THE SIBYL

The Sibyl was a prophetess. She could tell the future. For many years she wrote it all down on long scrolls.

Eventually she grew old. She wanted to stop recording the future. By then she had finished nine scrolls. She went to see King Tarquin in Rome. She offered to sell him the scrolls for a certain price. Tarquin, who was very proud, refused. He laughed at the old woman.

She set fire to three of the scrolls. She offered him the remaining scrolls. But the price had gone up. Tarquin was angry. He wanted to know the future, but now he had to pay more for fewer scrolls. He refused. She burned some more.

When there were just three scrolls left, Tarquin finally agreed to pay. The scrolls were put in a sacred shrine. His scribes read them whenever there was a problem in the state. But sometimes the scroll they needed was missing because it had been burned. They blamed Tarquin. Eventually they rebelled and overthrew him.

THE GEESE THAT SAVED ROME

Each of the gods had a favourite creature. Juno, queen of the gods, loved geese. Many of them waddled around her temple, hissing and honking. No one harmed them because they were sacred birds.

A savage tribe called the Gauls came to attack Rome. The Romans did not realize the danger they were in. Life had been peaceful for many years. Many of the soldiers had gone home to their families. There was no one to defend Rome.

One night the Gauls arrived at the foot of the Capitoline Hill. They were ready to rush in and capture the city. Suddenly, all the geese in Juno's temple started to cackle. The noise was so loud that everyone woke up. The generals quickly called their soldiers together. But the Gauls were terrified by the fierce birds and their terrible cackling. They had already started to run away.

The next morning, all the people gave thanks to Juno and her birds for saving the city.

CUPID AND PSYCHE

Cupid was the son of Venus, goddess of love. He was full of mischief. He always carried a bow and arrow. He fired arrows at people to make them fall in love with other people. This caused all kinds of trouble.

Venus was jealous of a beautiful mortal girl called Psyche. She sent Cupid to make her fall in love with the ugliest man alive. But instead Cupid fell in love with Psyche himself.

He visited her every night. He never let her light the lamps because he did not want her to recognize him. One night she disobeyed, and she saw Cupid. At once he ran away. Psyche searched for him all over the world. Jealous Venus created all kinds of problems for her, but Psyche overcame them all.

Eventually Cupid took pity on her. He asked Jupiter to make Psyche immortal so that they could be together for ever. He gave her a cup of ambrosia to drink and she joined the gods in heaven.

DIANA AND ACTAEON

Prince Actaeon, son of King Cadmus, loved to go out hunting. He had a wonderful pack of fierce hounds. All day he followed them as they ran through the woods chasing stags.

The goddess Diana had also been out hunting in the same woods. By evening she was hot and tired. She knew a secret pool hidden among the trees.

She took off her clothes and stepped into the cool water.

Suddenly, she felt someone was watching her. She looked up and saw Actaeon. The nymphs who were her servants gathered around her. They tried to hide her, but it was too late. Actaeon had seen the great goddess naked.

He tried to turn away but he could not move. He looked down. His feet were turning into hooves. Antlers were growing on his forehead. Diana had turned him into a stag. He heard the barking of his own hounds as they rushed at him. In a few seconds they had torn him to pieces.

BAUCIS AND PHILEMON

Jupiter and Mercury travelled the country in disguise, looking for people who were kind to strangers. They asked for shelter at many houses, but everyone turned them away. Eventually the two gods came to a cottage in the woods. An old couple, Baucis and Philemon, lived here. They were very poor. All they had was one goose, which laid eggs for them.

Baucis welcomed the strangers, but they had nothing to offer them for supper. They would have to kill their goose. Philemon went to catch it, but the goose recognized Jupiter and flew onto his knee. Then the gods took off their disguises. Jupiter transformed the cottage into a fine temple. In return for their kindness, he offered the old couple a reward.

But all Baucis and Philemon wanted was to look after the temple, and then to die together. When that time came, they were changed into two trees at the temple door. In time, the branches twined together, just like an old couple with their arms round each other.

PROSERPINA

Proserpina was the daughter of Ceres, goddess of agriculture, and Jupiter. One day she was in the fields picking flowers. Pluto, god of the underworld, saw her. He kidnapped her and took her down to the underworld to be his wife.

Ceres searched for Proserpina everywhere. Wherever she went the fruit and flowers stopped growing. The land became a desert. When he saw this, Jupiter sent Mercury to make Pluto set Proserpina free. Before Pluto let her go, he gave Proserpina six magic pomegranate seeds to eat. This meant she had to return to him every six months.

From then on, Proserpina lived half the year in the underworld. During that time it was cold winter on earth. In the springtime, Ceres decorated the earth with flowers to welcome her daughter back. They spent the summer happily together. But in the autumn, when Proserpina had to return to the underworld, everything started to die. The earth remained barren until next spring when she returned again.

ENDYMION AND THE MOON GODDESS

One evening, the goddess Diana was out hunting. She saw a shepherd boy sleeping on a hillside. His name was Endymion. He was the most handsome man she had ever seen. She bent down and kissed him.

When Endymion woke up, he thought it had all been a wonderful dream. The next night he went to sleep in the same place. He hoped it would happen again. Sure enough, when the moon came up, Diana returned and kissed him again. This went on for a long time.

Endymion lost interest in his real life. He longed for the night and his dreams.

One night Diana saw a grey hair in his head. She remembered that because he was mortal he must grow old, but she would always be young and beautiful.

She carried him away to Mount Latmos, the land of forgetfulness. She put a spell on him so that he would never wake up. Every night she visited him and he had the same lovely dream.

LARA THE CHATTERBOX

Lara was a river nymph. She was very beautiful, but she was a terrible chatterbox. She could never keep a secret.

One day she told everyone that Jupiter was in love with another nymph called Juturna. Jupiter's wife Juno was furious. To punish Lara, Jupiter pulled out her tongue and made her mute.

Jupiter told Mercury to take her down to the underworld. On the way there, they fell in love. They went to live in a cottage in the woods where they thought Jupiter would not find them. In time, Lara had two children. Mercury knew that Jupiter would try to harm the children. He made them invisible and sent them to live among humans.

Lara's children
became known as
the Lares, the
gods who
looked after the
household. Each
Roman family had
a little statue of them
in their home. At
mealtimes, they
always set an extra
place at the table in
case the invisible
children were there.

WHO'S WHO IN ROMAN MYTHS

AENEAS

A Trojan hero, Aeneas is the son of Venus and the mortal Anchises.

CERES

Ceres is the daughter of Saturn and mother of Proserpina. She is the goddess of corn and agriculture and is usually shown carrying a sheaf of corn. In Greek mythology she is called Demeter.

CUPID

He is the son of the goddess Venus and the god of love. Cupid is usually shown as a beautiful boy with a bow and quiver full of arrows. In Greek mythology he is called Eros.

DIANA

Daughter of Jupiter and Leto and twin sister of Apollo, Diana is the goddess of the moon, hunting and fertility. She is often shown wearing a knee-length pleated tunic and holding a bow and a quiver of arrows. Her special animals are hunting dogs and stags. In Greek mythology she is called Artemis.

JUNO

Juno is the queen of the gods. She is the wife (and sister) of Jupiter, sister of Neptune and Pluto, and mother of Mars and Vulcan. Her special bird is the peacock. In Greek mythology she is called Hera.

JUPITER

He is the ruler of the Roman gods, husband of Juno, son of Saturn and brother of Neptune, Pluto and Juno. As god of the sky, lightning and thunder, Jupiter is often shown holding a bolt of lightning. His special bird is the eagle. In Greek mythology he is called Zeus.

MARS

Son of Jupiter and Juno, Mars is the god of war. As the father of Romulus, the founder of Rome, Romans considered Mars almost as important as Jupiter. In Greek mythology he is called Ares.

MERCURY

Mercury is the son of Jupiter and Maia. He is the messenger god and protector of travellers and is usually shown wearing a winged helmet and boots with wings at the ankle. He holds a staff with two twined snakes. In Greek mythology he is called Hermes.

NEPTUNE

He is god of the sea and brother of Jupiter, Pluto and Juno. Neptune is usually shown travelling in a shell-shaped chariot drawn by creatures that are part-horse, part-dolphin. He holds a three-pointed spear called a trident. In Greek mythology he is called Poseidon.

ROMULUS AND REMUS

The twin sons of Mars and the mortal Rea Silva were raised by wolves and grew up to found Rome.

VENUS

The goddess of love and beauty, Venus was born from the sea and is sometimes shown standing in a seashell. In Greek mythology she is called Aphrodite.

GLOSSARY

agriculture The business of growing crops.

ambrosia The food and drink of the gods.

Capitoline The highest and most important of the seven hills of Rome.

Carthage An ancient city in North Africa, near present-day Tunis.

empire A collection of lands under the control of a single ruler.

Etruscans An ancient people living in central Italy.

Gauls An ancient people whose lands included France and northern Italy.

immortal Someone who lives forever.

Lethe The river separating the earth from the underworld.

mortal Human.

mosaic A picture made up of tiny pieces of coloured stone.

nymph A nature spirit, usually a young girl.

pomegranate A fruit with many red, juicy seeds.

prophecy A prediction of a future event.

sacrifice To kill an animal as an offering to the gods.

scroll A roll of parchment.

sybil A kind of priestess who could tell the future.

temple A place of worship.

Tiber The river that passes through Rome.

Titans A race of godlike giants.

underworld According to ancient myths, the place beneath the earth where the souls of the dead go.

whitethorn The hawthorn bush.

FURTHER INFORMATION

BOOKS

Classic Myths to read Aloud: the Great Stories of Greek and Roman Mythology by William F Russell (Three Rivers Press, 1992)

Greek and Roman Mythology by Don Nardo (Lucent Books, 1997)

Greek and Roman Mythology A-Z by Kathleen N Daly and Marian Rengel (Facts on File, 2003)

Mythology: Timeless Tales of Gods and Heroes by Edith Hamilton (Grand Central Publishing, 1999)

Myths and Civilisation of the Ancient Romans by John Malam (Peter Bedrick Books, 1999)

Roman Mythology by Joy Paige (Rosen, 2006)

Roman Mythology by Evelyn Wolfson (Enslow, 2003)

Roman Myths by Geraldine McCaughrean (Margaret K McElderry, 2001)

Stories from Ancient Civilisations: Rome by Shahrukh Husain (Evans, 2004)

The World Mythology Series: Heroes, Gods and Emperors from Roman Mythology by Kerry Usher (Peter Bedrick Books, 1992)

WEBSITES

www.novaroma.org/religio_romana/deities.html
An introduction to Roman religion

www.42explore2.com/rome.htm
A guide to ancient Rome, with links to other websites

www.angelfire.com/geek/romanmyth/
A website on Roman gods, goddesses and myths

www.unrv.com/culture/mythology.php
All aspects of Roman history are covered here, including Roman religion and myths

www.online-mythology.com
A collection of Greek and Roman myths

INDEX